# KIDS ASK™
# Who?

Illustrations by Marilee Harrald-Pilz

Publications International, Ltd.

# Who puts the holes in cheese?

Kids Ask is a trademark of Publications International, Ltd.

Copyright © 2007 Publications International, Ltd.
All rights reserved. This book may not be reproduced or quoted in whole
or in part by any means whatsoever without written permission from:

Louis Weber, CEO
Publications International, Ltd.
7373 North Cicero Avenue
Lincolnwood, Illinois 60712

Permission is never granted for commercial purposes.

Dubble Bubble® is a registered trademark of Tootsie Roll Industries, Inc.
Play-doh® is a registered trademark of Hasbro, Inc.
Crayola® is a registered trademark of Binney & Smith Properties, Inc.

ISBN-13: 978-1-4127-8944-8
ISBN-10: 1-4127-8944-3

Manufactured in China.

8 7 6 5 4 3 2 1

Who invented Play-doh?

# Contents

Who created Halloween?

# Who invented sandwiches?

The sandwich was invented more than 200 years ago by a man named John Montagu. He lived in a town called Sandwich, England. He liked to play cards so much that he didn't even want to stop to eat. So he put a piece of meat between two pieces of bread so he could eat and still play. His idea caught on with other people, and the sandwich was born.

Lisa

mountain water

yogurt

# Who puts the holes in cheese?

Cheesemakers put holes in Swiss cheese by adding a harmless bacteria to the cheese. When the cheese and bacteria are warmed up, air bubbles are formed. These bubbles pop, leaving holes in the cheese.

## FUN FACT

The holes in Swiss cheese are called *eyes*. Swiss cheese without holes is called *blind*.

# Who was the first President of the United States?

George Washington was the first President of the United States. He was one of the most famous presidents ever. His picture is on the one dollar bill and the quarter.

## FUN FACT

It is believed that Betsy Ross sewed America's first flag. It had 13 stars and 13 red and white stripes for the 13 original states. It was flown when the Declaration of Independence was first read in July 1776.

# Who are the presidents shown on Mount Rushmore?

The faces of George Washington, Thomas Jefferson, Theodore Roosevelt, and Abraham Lincoln are carved into the side of Mount Rushmore in South Dakota. Each face is 60 feet tall! Gutzon Borglum and 400 workers created the monument. They worked on and off for more than six and a half years from 1927 to 1941.

# Who invented television?

V. K. Zworykin made the very first television in 1920. When television was new, there were only about 150 TV sets in the United States. Today, just about everybody has at least one TV. The first TV sets were very small. They showed only black-and-white pictures. Usually, the sound and picture were not very clear.

# Who creates video games?

Video game designers create video games. They are artists who like to draw and design things on computers. And they usually love to play video games!

## FUN FACT

Thomas Edison invented the electric lightbulb in 1879. Before that, people used candles and lamps that burned gas to see in the dark. Thomas Edison also invented the phonograph, a machine that played back recorded music long before CDs or MP3 players were ever dreamed of!

# Who built the Great Wall of China?

The Great Wall of China began as many smaller walls. These walls were built to protect against attacks. A Chinese ruler decided to link the walls together more than 2,000 years ago. In all, it took more than 300,000 people to build the Great Wall.

## FUN FACT

The Great Wall of China is about 4,000 miles long. That's as far as the distance from Chicago to Paris.

# Who invented the circus?

In ancient Rome thousands of years ago, people would go to the circus to see exotic animals, horse and chariot races, and gladiator battles. The type of circus we know today originated in 1768, when Philip Astley held the first circus in London, England. It had acrobats, horses, a tightrope walker, and a clown named Burt.

## FUN FACT

On a very hot day at the 1904 World's Fair in St. Louis, an ice cream seller ran out of dishes. His customers were getting very angry. A waffle-maker heard this, so he brought over some waffles. They rolled up the waffles, put the ice cream on top, and the ice-cream cone was born!

# Who invented cotton candy?

When cotton candy was first introduced in the mid-18th century, it was called *fairy floss*. It was very expensive and took a long time to make. In 1897, William Morrison and John Wharton invented an electric machine to quickly melt and spin sugar into the sticky treat. After that, cotton candy became popular at carnivals and fairs and in candy stores.

# Who flew the first airplane?

Brothers Wilbur and Orville Wright made the first flight in a real airplane. On December 17, 1903, they flew their plane, *The Flyer,* at Kitty Hawk, North Carolina. The plane went 120 feet in 12 seconds. Their next flight was even better. The plane flew 852 feet and stayed in the air for almost a minute!

## FUN FACT

Amelia Earhart was a famous aviator of the 1930s. In 1932, she became the first woman to fly across the Atlantic Ocean alone. In 1937, Amelia tried to fly around the world. But her plane disappeared in the South Pacific and was never found.

# Who was Dr. Seuss?

Dr. Seuss is the best-selling children's author of all time. His real name was Theodor Seuss Geisel, but he wrote under the name Dr. Seuss. He wasn't a real doctor; he was a writer and a cartoonist. He was best known for his children's books, including *Green Eggs and Ham, The Cat in the Hat,* and *How the Grinch Stole Christmas!* Which one is your favorite?

## FUN FACT

Before he became an author of children's books, Theodor Geisel made training movies for the U.S. Army during World War II.

# Who created Halloween?

Halloween started a few thousand years ago with the ancient Celts (a group of people who worshipped nature). For them, October 31 was the end of the year, so they threw a big party. During this celebration, they believed spirits could come back and visit with living relatives. Some people believed that if you left treats on the front porch for the spirits and ghosts, this would make them happy, and they wouldn't hurt you. So treats became part of the Halloween tradition. Trick or treat!

# Who invented bubble gum?

People have chewed forms of gum for thousands of years. Then, in 1928, a man named Walter Diemer created the first bubble gum. This pink chewing gum was called *Dubble Bubble*, and it is still made today.

## FUN FACT

According to an Irish legend, Jack O'Lantern was a lost soul who appeared at night as a ghost. To keep Jack and other spirits away, Irish people carved scary faces into potatoes and turnips. When Irish people came to America in the 18th and 19th centuries, they started carving scary faces into pumpkins instead, and the jack-o'-lantern as we know it came to be.

# Who was the first person to walk on the moon?

American astronaut Neil Armstrong was the first person to set foot on the moon. When he landed on July 20, 1969, he said, "That's one small step for man, one giant leap for mankind." Together, Armstrong and fellow astronaut Buzz Aldrin placed an American flag on the surface of the moon. As far as we know, it's still there.

## FUN FACT

When there is a full moon, some people think they see a face on the moon. We call this the Man in the Moon. But nobody really lives on the moon. The "face" is formed by mountains and craters (big holes) on the surface of the moon.

# Who is Jack Frost?

Have you ever woken up on a very cold morning and found pretty patterns of ice on the windows? People sometimes say that it was Jack Frost who made the icy patterns on the windows. But Jack Frost isn't a real person. It is just a name made up to explain where ice and frost come from.

# Who is Mother Nature?

It can be hard to explain how some things come to be, such as the change of seasons, the growth of flowers, or even bad weather such as tornadoes. Sometimes people will say that Mother Nature is responsible for these things. But like Jack Frost, Mother Nature isn't a real person.

# Who invented Play-doh?

Joseph and Noah McVicker invented a special type of modeling clay in 1956. They called it Play-doh. There was originally only one color—off-white—but today Play-doh comes in many colors. More than 700 million pounds of Play-doh have been sold, but the recipe remains a secret.

Modeling Dough

Modeling Dough

# Who invented crayons?

In 1902, Edwin Binney and Harold Smith invented the type of crayons you use today. They combined a special kind of wax with dyes to create the first Crayola crayons. Today, Crayola crayons come in 120 different colors.

# Who was Helen Keller?

Helen Keller was born in 1880. When she was just a baby, a terrible disease left her blind, deaf, and unable to speak. Can you imagine that? When Helen was seven, Anne Sullivan became her teacher. One day, Anne poured water on Helen's hand then wrote the letters *W-A-T-E-R* in her palm. Helen finally understood, and she learned many other words that day. Helen went to college, learned to read 5 languages in braille, and wrote 11 books in her lifetime. She also gave speeches and raised money to help other blind people.

**FUN FACT**

Braille is a special kind of writing that uses raised dots to help blind people read.

w a t e r

# Who were the Pilgrims?

The Pilgrims were English colonists who came to America in 1620. They wanted more freedom than they had in their former country. Their first winter in the new land was very hard, and they didn't have enough food to eat. But native people showed them how to grow crops and hunt. When the Pilgrims were sure they would have enough food to last the winter, they invited the native people to a big feast. They ate turkey, vegetables, and pumpkin pie. This was the first Thanksgiving dinner.

## FUN FACT

Pocahontas was a Native American princess born in 1595. Legend has it that she saved the life of a colonist named Captain John Smith. She later married a man named John Rolfe and moved to England. These actions helped keep peace between the Native Americans and the colonists for many years.

# Who created basketball?

Dr. James Naismith, a physical education teacher in Massachusetts, invented the game of basketball in 1891. He was asked to create a game that would distract the energetic students who were stuck inside during the cold winter. Today, basketball is a game played by more than 300 million people worldwide. That's more than all the people who live in the United States!

**FUN FACT**

Not only did James Naismith create the game of basketball, he also invented the football helmet.

31

# Who makes sure my suitcase gets on the right airplane?

When you check in at an airport, you leave your suitcase at the counter. The person behind the counter puts a tag on it that tells the baggage handlers where you (and your suitcase!) are going. A baggage handler reads the ticket and loads the suitcase onto the right airplane. When the airplane lands, baggage handlers at that airport unload your suitcase. You can identify it by the tag. Bon voyage!